Hocus Pocus Stir & Cook
The Kitchen Science
Magic Book

D1450251

James Lewis

Meadowbrook Press
Distributed by Simon & Schuster
New York

To my wife, Nancy, and my two children, Tiffany and Jared

Library of Congress Cataloging-in-Publication Data

Lewis, James, 1943–
     Hocus pocus stir and cook: the kitchen science magic book / James Lewis
          p.   cm.
     Summary: Scientific experiments that produce a "magic" effect and that can be done in the kitchen.
     ISBN 0-88166-183-X
     1. Science—Experiments—Juvenile literature. [1. Science—Experiments. 2. Experiments.] I. Title.
Q164.L478 1991   91-30403
507.8—dc20   CIP
                                                                          AC

S&S Ordering #: 0-671-74767-3

© 1991 by James Lewis

All rights reserved. No part of this book may be reproduced in any form without permission from the publisher, except in the case of brief quotations embodied in critical articles and reviews.

Editor: Katherine Stevenson
Illustrator: Rebecca Hirsch

Published by Meadowbrook Press, 18318 Minnetonka Boulevard, Deephaven, MN 55391.

BOOK TRADE DISTRIBUTION by Simon & Schuster, a division of Simon and Schuster, Inc., 1230 Avenue of the Americas, New York, NY 10020.

95 94 93 92 91   5 4 3 2 1

Printed in the United States of America

Disclaimer:
Adult supervision is advised when working with certain activities in this book. No responsibility is implied or taken for anyone who sustains injuries as a result of using the materials or ideas put forward in this book. Follow the step-by-step procedures and avoid shortcuts. Use the safe materials specified. Never work alone when an adult helper is recommended. Safety precautions are noted for each activity. If you use common sense and make safety the first consideration, you will enjoy a safe, fun, educational, and rewarding science activity.

Contents

Preface

Adults may use the kitchen to cook meals, but kids can use it to investigate and experiment. There is no need for kids to buy an expensive chemistry set when pots and pans, baking soda, and vinegar are available in their own kitchen "laboratory." With simple experiments and inexpensive materials, kids can explore the magic of atmospheric pressure, pH factor, and the Bernoulli principle, making their world understandable. They can learn to vary experiments to get different results or find different ways to obtain the same results. They can even gain insight from failure. The lure of every science experiment becomes the scientific process—hypothesizing and investigating—not just seeing results.

Even though many of these activities can be done by kids alone, adult supervision is critical. The adult helper guarantees safety when necessary and acts as coach, asking questions and suggesting alternatives—but not giving away results! Adult participation conveys to kids that the scientific process is not only important and educational, but also enjoyable and rewarding.

I thank the people who encouraged me during the writing of this book and its three predecessors, including the staff at Centennial Elementary School and other schools in the Springfield School District, and the Springfield Public Library. A special thanks goes to the local bookstore owners and managers who have publicized these books. I also thank my family for giving me the time to write and for sacrificing their needs to support mine. Finally, thank you to all the elementary school teachers and science book authors who help make the study of science so exciting for children.

Note to Kids

Making Kitchen Science Safe

1. **Be sure to get an adult helper for the activities in part two, With an Adult.** These activities use glass, knives, objects with pointed or sharp edges, small objects that are easy to swallow, open flame, or electrical appliances. Look for the With an Adult notice at the top of each page.

2. **Ask your adult helper's permission before using any kitchen ingredients, utensils, or appliances.** Each item in the kitchen has a specific use and should not be used as a toy.

3. **Plan ahead by reading the activity first, then assembling all the supplies you'll need.** (Don't read the What Did You See? and Why Did It Happen? sections, though, or you'll spoil the surprise!)

4. **Clean materials thoroughly before you use them, including removing any residues from the insides of containers.** Don't use containers that were used to hold medicines or cleaners. Avoid using containers with sharp edges.

5. **Wear an old shirt or an apron to keep your clothes clean.** Food coloring and some other materials used in the activities can stain clothes.

6. **Make sure you have a safe, comfortable way to reach cupboards and the kitchen counter.** A sturdy step stool provides extra height safely.

7. **Wash your hands before each activity or anytime they get dirty.** Clean hands are necessary when handling food and provide a safe grip on other materials.

8. **Keep all chemicals off your skin and out of your mouth!** Even fairly safe chemicals such as vinegar or baking soda should be handled with care.

9. **Keep all chemicals and dangerous materials out of the reach of younger children.** And when you finish an activity, put all chemicals, ingredients, and clean utensils back where they belong.

10. **To avoid burns, use pot holders whenever you move anything that might be hot.** Always test the hot water from the kitchen faucet with your finger before you place your whole hand in it.

11. **Clean up after each activity so the kitchen will be safe and usable.** Carefully wipe up any wet spots on the floor so you don't slip.

12. **Prepare for the unexpected.** These activities are planned with safety in mind, but be willing to get help and postpone an activity if an accident should occur.

Note to Parents

1. The activities in this book are designed for children of elementary school age. Although your children can read and perform many of the activities independently, you, as parents, should supervise and assist in the activities for both educational and safety reasons.

2. The activities in part two, With an Adult, use heat, open flame, chemicals, or sharp objects and must be supervised closely. They are designed to be performed with parental help and in specific areas of the kitchen. Look for the With an Adult notice at the top of the page.

3. The instructions in each activity are written at an elementary-school reading level. However, you might wish to read the directions first and rephrase them for your children, especially if they have difficulty reading the words or understanding the steps.

4. Most activities are designed to take only five minutes; however, others might take a week to show the results. Encourage your children to be patient and try other activities while waiting.

5. Let your children repeat an activity. One brief exposure to a new idea might not satisfy their curiosity.

6. Encourage your children to try the variations listed with many activities. Varying an activity—using different ingredients, for example—can provide greater understanding of the concept presented. (Variations of activities that require heat or flame still must be closely supervised.)

7. Always encourage your children to explain what happens in each activity, but don't demand answers or turn the activities into drills. Let your children enjoy them! Motivating your children to explain things in their own words will foster their understanding of science concepts. You can help by paraphrasing their responses and showing them how to use new words and explore new concepts.

8. The materials you'll need are listed in each activity and in a master list at the beginning of the book. You'll find most of the materials in your home, but some (marked with asterisks) might require a quick trip to the store.

Materials

Kitchen Supplies:
Aluminum soft drink cans
Baking pan
Bottle (glass)
Bowls (various sizes)
Dishpan (or large bowl)
Dish towel
Drinking glasses (plastic)
Food cans (unopened)
Jars (glass & plastic)
Knife (sharp)
Measuring cup & spoons
Milk carton (1 quart or
 1 liter)
Oven mitts
Paper cup (unwaxed)
Paper towel
Pie plates (metal & glass)
Plastic wrap
Pot holders
Saucepan (with lid)
Scale
Soft drink bottles (clear
 plastic & glass)
Spoons (plastic & metal)
Strainer
Straws
Table knife
Teakettle
Tin foil
Tongs (metal)
Toothpick
Wine glass or glass goblet
Wooden mixing spoon

Kitchen Ingredients:
Baking soda
Cooking oil
Food coloring
Fruit or vegetable juices
Ice cubes
Pepper
Salt
Sugar
Vinegar (white or red)
*Yeast

Optional:
Cinnamon
Flour
Grape, beet, or cranberry
 juice
Lemon juice
Nutmeg

Household Supplies:
Ammonia
Ballpoint pen
Bleach (liquid chlorine)
Books
Candleholder
Candles
*Cork (to fit soft drink
 bottle)
*Cotton string
*Eyedropper
*Funnels (two, same size,
 plastic or metal)
Index cards
*Ink (washable)
*Laundry bluing
*Magnifying glass
Matches
Nail
Newspaper
Paintbrush (small water-
 color)
Pencil
Pliers
Pocket mirrors
Rubbing alcohol
Ruler
Scissors
Sponge
Straight pin
*Tape (plastic, electrical, &
 duct)
*Wire (fine)
Wool cloth
Writing paper
Yardsticks (metersticks)
 or broom handles

Optional:
Alka-Seltzer
Bleach powdered,
 nonchlorinated
Buttons
Cardboard tube
Paper clips

Foods:
Apples
Butter or margarine
Eggs
Meat bones
Popcorn
Raisins
*Red cabbage

Optional:
Grapes
Milk
Potato
Soda pop

Miscellaneous:
Balloons
Charcoal or coal
Pennies
Plastic bag with tie
Rocks (porous)
Twigs

Optional:
Ball
Dime
*Glitter

***Items that might require
a quick trip to the store.**

By Yourself

Pepper Pick-up

Can you pick up pepper with the *back* of a spoon?

Let's Find Out:

Say you've spilled some salt and pepper on the table. How could you pick it up? You could brush it off, or wipe it up with a sponge, but those methods are pretty boring. Do you think you could pick up *just the pepper*, leaving the salt? You can, believe it or not, with the back of a spoon!

What You Need:

A shallow bowl; pepper; salt; a plastic spoon; a piece of wool cloth. *Optional:* sugar; cinnamon; flour; nutmeg.

What to Do:

1. Start by pouring some salt and pepper into a shallow bowl.

2. Mix the salt and pepper together with your finger.

3. Place a plastic spoon over the salt and pepper—close to the bowl but not touching it. What happens? Now rub a plastic spoon on a wool cloth while you slowly count to 15.

4. Hold the spoon over the salt and pepper again. Look underneath the spoon to see what happens. Shake the pepper that jumps to the spoon into another bowl and try it again!

What Did You See?

The pepper jumped to the spoon after you rubbed the spoon on the wool cloth.

Why Did It Happen?

The plastic spoon becomes charged with static electricity when you rub it on the wool cloth. The spoon acts like a magnet and pulls the light pieces of pepper to it. Holding the spoon really close might catch some of the salt grains (which are heavier), too.

Variation:

Try using other combinations, such as sugar and cinnamon or flour and nutmeg.

Spoon Nose

Can you hang a spoon from the end of your nose?

Let's Find Out:

People sometimes set pencils above their ears or prop their sunglasses on top of their head. But have you ever seen someone hang a spoon from his or her nose? Let's see if you can do it!

What You Need:

A metal teaspoon. *Optional:* a plastic spoon; a metal tablespoon.

What to Do:

1. Take a metal teaspoon, press the bowl of it over the end of your nose with the handle hanging downward, and let go. Does it stay?

2. Now rub the bowl of the teaspoon with your fingers until it's warm. (Or you can hold it in warm water. Be sure to dry it.)

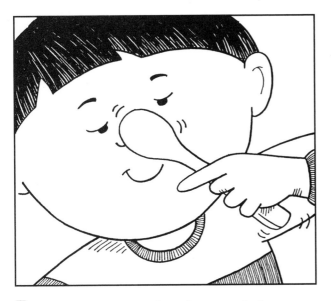

3. Rub the warm bowl up and down on the end of your nose.

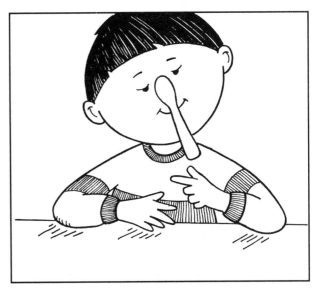

4. When the spoon feels like it's starting to stick, tilt your head back a little and let go. How long can you keep it there? Why do you think it stays there? Try it again.

What Did You See?

When the teaspoon was cold it would not stick to your nose, but when it was warm it stuck there for a little while.

Why Did It Happen?

Nobody knows for sure what makes the spoon stick! Some think the warmed spoon causes your skin to produce more oil. The oil, which is somewhat sticky, may keep the spoon attached by *friction* for a short while. Others think that the nose begins to take on the shape of the spoon. Still others think a vacuum forms in the tiny space between the spoon and the nose.

Variation:

Try using a plastic spoon or a metal tablespoon.

Dinner Music

Can you make music using dinner glasses?

Let's Find Out:

You've probably tapped the side of a glass with a spoon to make a bell-like sound. But can you think of a way to make another musical sound with a glass . . . using only your finger? Check with your parents first about which glasses are OK to use—and when it's OK to be noisy!

What You Need:

A thin-walled drinking glass, wine glass, or glass goblet. *Optional:* cooking oil; vinegar.

What to Do:

1. Fill a thin glass with water. (Make sure the glass doesn't have any cracks or chips on the rim!)

2. Hold the glass steady with one hand. Dip a fingertip of your other hand into the water. (Your finger can't be too wet or too dry, or this activity won't work.)

3. *Lightly* rub your finger in a circular motion around the rim of the glass. What happens? Vary the pressure a bit to see what difference it makes. *Be careful—use only slight pressure!*

4. Try putting more (or less) water in the glass. What happens? Which water level makes the nicest sound?

What Did You See?

Rubbing your finger around the rim of the glass made a ringing sound. The pitch of the sound depended on the amount of water in the glass.

Why Did It Happen?

Your finger doesn't move smoothly on the rim of the glass; instead it catches and slips in a series of little jerks. This jerking motion causes the glass to vibrate and make a sound. Some musical instruments, like the violin, work in the same way. The hairs on the bow catch and jerk on the strings and make the strings vibrate, producing sounds.

Variations:

1. Try making the sound with a drop of cooking oil on the tip of your finger.
2. Try it (using a clean glass) with vinegar on the tip of your finger.

Strange Music

Can you play a paper cup like an instrument?

Let's Find Out:

A string stretched over a box or wood frame is the simplest version of a stringed instrument. When an object such as a bow or guitar pick rubs or strikes the string, it vibrates and the instrument makes sounds. Likewise, a paper cup can be used to make sounds— but you'll have to decide whether those sounds are sweet!

What You Need:

A paper cup (any size); a toothpick; a piece of thin cotton string 18 to 24 inches (45 to 60 centimeters) long; a paper towel. *Optional:* different-sized paper cups.

What to Do:

1. Use a toothpick to make a tiny hole in the bottom of a paper cup.

2. Carefully push one end of a cotton string through the hole and into the cup. (It helps to use the toothpick to push the string through the hole.)

3. Tie the string around the middle of the toothpick. Pull the string back through the cup, and break the ends of the toothpick so it fits in the bottom of the cup.

4. Wet a paper towel, and wrap it around the string near the cup. Squeeze the paper towel on the string, and pull it away from the cup. What happens?

What Did You See?

Pulling the paper towel along the string made a loud squawking sound.

Why Did It Happen?

Rubbing the paper towel on the string makes vibrations, which travel along the string to the toothpick pressed against the bottom of the cup. The toothpick passes the vibrations on to the bottom and sides of the cup, making the vibrations bigger and louder. The cup acts like a loudspeaker, a megaphone, or like holding your hands around your mouth when you yell.

Variation:

Try different-sized paper cups.

Against the Wind

When is still, quiet air stronger than moving air?

Let's Find Out:

You've seen the direct pressure of the wind push against the sail of a boat and propel it rapidly through the water. But what happens when air blows between two objects? Will it push them apart?

What You Need:

12 to 24 plastic drinking straws of the same size (perfectly round, not crushed or bent); 2 empty aluminum soft drink cans; a ruler.

What to Do:

1. Arrange some straws side by side, with a little space between them, on the kitchen counter. Make sure the kitchen counter is smooth and dry and that the straws roll freely.

2. Stand two empty soft drink cans a little distance apart, on the straws. See how the straws act like rollers under them?

3. What do you think would happen if you blew gently between the cans? Try it and see what happens.

4. Move the cans farther apart and blow again. How far apart can you put the cans and still blow them together? Measure the distance between the cans with a ruler each time before you blow.

What Did You See?

When you blew between the cans, they moved together. When you moved the cans too far apart, however, blowing between them no longer moved them together.

Why Did It Happen?

Fast-moving air, like the air you blew between the cans, pushes away air molecules, lowering air pressure. This phenomenon is called the *Bernoulli Principle*. The air outside the cans, which does not move, still has normal air pressure and pushes the cans together. Moving air, like the wind, *feels* stronger than calm, quiet air, but in many cases it is not. Moving air is "stronger" when it hits something head-on but is less strong when it moves *through* an area, lowering the air pressure.

Fuller Than Full

Can you add pennies to a full glass of water without making it overflow?

Let's Find Out:

Usually something that's full is *full!* You can't add anything more to it without taking something out. When a glass of water is filled to the brim, it should be full. But is it?

What You Need:

A clear plastic drinking glass; an eyedropper; lots of pennies. *Optional:* lots of paper clips or buttons.

What to Do:

1. Fill a dry plastic glass almost to the brim with water, and set it on the kitchen counter.

2. Take a good look from the side of the glass, and use an eyedropper to add more water—carefully!—until the water is exactly even with the top of the glass. What do you think will happen if you add a penny to this full glass of water?

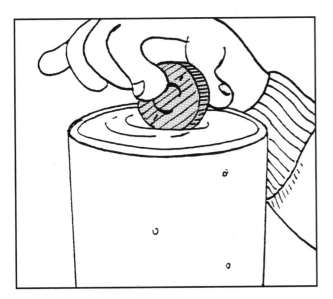

3. Put a penny in slowly and carefully . . . but don't make a splash! Watch what happens. Check the sides of the glass carefully to see if any water spilled out.

4. Start adding more pennies, one at a time. After each one, check the side of the glass and the top of the water. What is happening? How many pennies can you add to the glass before the water spills out?

What Did You See?

As you added pennies to the glass, no water spilled out. Instead, the top surface of the water bulged upward. Finally, the water spilled over the sides.

Why Did It Happen?

As you add pennies, the water in the glass bulges but doesn't spill because the tiny particles of water on and near the surface hold onto each other strongly. The surface stretches upward like a balloon until the weight of the water above the rim of the glass is so great, it breaks and spills over the side. The tendency for water molecules to cling together and create the bulge above the rim is called *surface tension*.

Variation:

Empty and dry the glass, and try again using paper clips or buttons instead of pennies.

Restless Raisins

Can you make sunken raisins float—without touching them?

Let's Find Out:

Do you know what happens to the raisins in your cereal when you pour milk on them? They're heavy enough to sink in milk and in water, too. Once they've sunk, can you think of a way to raise them up again—without touching them? All it takes is two simple kitchen chemicals.

What You Need:

A tall clear plastic drinking glass; a tablespoon (15 milliliters) measure; baking soda; vinegar; 4 or 5 raisins. *Optional:* Alka-Seltzer; unpopped popcorn; grapes; buttons.

What to Do:

1. Fill a tall plastic drinking glass three-fourths full with water.

2. Add a tablespoon (15 milliliters) of baking soda to the water. Stir until the water is clear again.

3. Drop 4 or 5 raisins in the water. What happens?

4. Now pour 2 to 4 tablespoons (30 to 60 milliliters) of vinegar into the glass. What happens to the raisins? Add more vinegar to get plenty of action. How long do the raisins float before they sink again?

What Did You See?

The raisins sank to the bottom of the water and baking soda solution. But adding the vinegar made lots of bubbles, some of which stuck to the raisins and floated them to the surface. When the bubbles popped, the raisins sank again.

Why Did It Happen?

Mixing vinegar (an acid) and baking soda (a base) together forms a gas called carbon dioxide (CO_2). Bubbles of carbon dioxide stick to the sides of the raisins because a raisin's skin tends to repel water and allow the CO_2 gas to attach. The bubbles act like air bags and float the heavy raisins to the surface. At the surface, the bubbles break and the raisins sink again.

Variations:

1. Try using other fizzy liquids to float the raisins, such as clear soda pop or Alka-Seltzer in water.

2. Try floating items like unpopped popcorn, grapes (both peeled and un-peeled), and buttons.

The Swimming Egg

Can you make an egg float in water?

Let's Find Out:

When you go swimming, you are able to float in the water if you keep air in your lungs. But did you know you can float more easily in salt water, like the ocean, than in fresh water? Eggs aren't usually Olympic-class swimmers, but if you follow these steps you can make one float really well!

What You Need:

A wide-mouthed quart (liter) glass jar; salt (kosher or pickling salt makes the water more clear); a tablespoon (15 milliliters) measure; a spoon; a fresh egg; a small cup measure. *Optional:* a potato.

What to Do:

1. Fill a wide-mouthed quart (liter) jar half full with water. Carefully place an egg in the water. What happens? An egg must not have much air inside or else it would float!

2. Remove the egg carefully and stir 2 to 3 tablespoons (30 to 45 milliliters) of salt into the water. Now place the egg in the salt water. What happens? Add more salt, stirring *gently* with a spoon, until the egg floats to the surface.

3. Carefully pour cold tap water from a small cup measure down the *side* of the container. *Don't* add the water quickly or pour it in the middle of the salt water! (Tipping the jar might help.) What happens?

4. Keep adding tap water to make the egg settle to the middle of the jar. Can you make it sink to the bottom?

What Did You See?

The egg sank in the tap water but floated to the surface when you added enough salt. It floated with the large, rounded end up. The egg floated in the middle of the jar after you added tap water.

Why Did It Happen?

A fresh raw egg has an air sac at the large rounded end, but the sac is too small to make the egg float in tap (fresh) water. Only when the egg gets old and stale does the air sac get large enough to float the egg. Salt water, however, is heavier or *denser* than plain water, and better supports the weight of the egg. Carefully adding more tap water forms a layer of lighter or *less dense* water on top of the salt water. The egg sinks through the lighter water but stops at the salt water.

Variation:

Try using a section of a raw, peeled potato instead of an egg . . . carve it into the shape of a small starfish, sea horse, or whale for fun!

Under Pressure

Can you make eggshells support books without breaking?

Let's Find Out:

Eggshells seem pretty fragile . . . just think how easily they break if you drop them! So, do you think you can make eggshells hold weight—as much weight as a stack of books? It's just a matter of knowing how!

What You Need:

Four medium-sized fresh eggs; a teaspoon; a bowl; plastic or electrical tape; scissors; books; a kitchen scale (or, if you don't have one, a bathroom scale).

What to Do:

1. Remove the yolk and white from four fresh eggs by tapping carefully with a teaspoon around one end of each egg to make a small hole.

2. Dump the yolks and whites into a bowl . . . then rinse and dry the eggshells. (Cover the yolks and whites and put them in the refrigerator—you can use them to make an omelette or scrambled eggs later.)

3. Wrap tape around the middle of each eggshell, keeping the tape straight. Using scissors, cut away the broken end of each shell right up to the tape line. Try to make sure all the eggshells are the same height when you stand them on the cut edges—they should look like they've been cut in half.

4. Set the four eggshells on the kitchen counter, just like the legs of a table, and try to guess how many books they might hold. Add books—*gently*—until the shells finally crack. How many books did they hold? Weigh the books on a kitchen scale to find out how heavy they were.

What Did You See?

The eggshells were easy to cut with scissors, but they did not crack easily when you piled books on them. Eventually they cracked after you stacked several books on them.

Why Did It Happen?

Eggshells are very thin and are made of calcium, the same substance that makes up bone. Their strength comes from their shape—a dome. Domes are very strong because any weight pushing down from the top is spread equally to all the points around the bottom. Some very large buildings, such as sports arenas, have dome-shaped roofs that cover large areas without any center supports.

It's Alive

Can you inflate a balloon—without blowing a single breath?

Let's Find Out:

You don't usually think of kitchen ingredients as being alive, but one is—it's in a *dormant* or inactive stage, like a hibernating bear. The ingredient is yeast. When combined with other simple kitchen ingredients, yeast grows and triggers some very interesting chemical reactions.

What You Need:

A jar; a packet of active dry yeast (¼ ounce or 7 grams); a ½-cup (⅛-liter) measure; a 1-cup (¼-liter) measure; sugar; a spoon for stirring; a funnel; a glass soft drink bottle; a balloon that has already been stretched or inflated at least once. *Optional:* ½ cup (⅛ liter) of flour.

What to Do:

1. Let's start growing some yeast. Fill a jar with 1 cup (¼ liter) of warm—but not hot—water. Then add the contents of one packet of active dry yeast.

2. Add ½ cup (⅛ liter) of sugar, and stir the mixture with a spoon.

3. Using the funnel, pour half the contents of the jar into a glass soft drink bottle.

4. Cover the bottle with a stretched-out balloon, and leave the other half of the yeast mixture in the jar. Now check the two containers over the next hour. What happens to the mixture in the jar? What happens to the balloon?

What Did You See?

In both containers the yeast mixture created a foam that rose above the water level. The balloon covering the bottle inflated!

Why Did It Happen?

When mixed with water, the dried yeast plants absorb the water and come to life. Then they start to eat the sugar and give off a waste made up of alcohol and carbon dioxide gas. This water-sugar-yeast combination is what you mix with flour to make bread: the carbon dioxide forms the little holes you see in the bread, and the alcohol evaporates when the bread gets hot.

Variation:

Try adding ½ cup (⅛ liter) of flour to the water-sugar-yeast mixture in step 2.

Antigravity Machine

Can you roll two funnels uphill without pushing them?

Let's Find Out:

If you think rolling a ball uphill without pushing it would be tough . . . then think about rolling two *funnels* up a hill. Impossible? Maybe not, if you know how. (And once you know how to do this trick with funnels, maybe you will figure out how to roll a *ball* uphill.)

What You Need:

Two funnels (the same size, either plastic or metal); plastic or electrical tape; some cookbooks or other large books; 2 yardsticks (metersticks) or broom handles. *Optional:* a ball similar in size to the funnels.

What to Do:

1. Take 2 same-sized funnels and tape the large ends together neatly. Don't let the tape stick out too far from the rims.

2. Place 2 large books on the kitchen counter, table, or floor and 3 more books about a yard (meter) away. The stack of 3 books must be higher than the stack of 2 books.

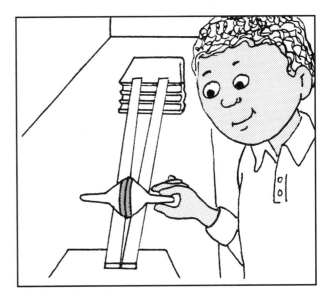

3. Place 2 yardsticks (metersticks) or broom handles so they stretch from one pile of books to the other. The sticks should form a V-shaped track, with the point of the V on the lower stack of books.

4. Place the funnels at the low end of the track, in the point of the V, and let them go. Can you get them to roll up the hill? Watch the funnels carefully, looking to see whether the *center* of each cone is actually going uphill or downhill.

What Did You See?

The funnels traveled from the low end to the high end of the track and stayed there. The center of the cone, however, traveled downhill.

Why Did It Happen?

Each funnel tapers from a big end to a small end. The biggest part of the funnel touches the sticks first. As the track widens, the funnels actually drop down into the tracks because of their sloping sides. The funnels look like they are going uphill, but they are really traveling *downhill*. They only give the illusion of rolling uphill!

Variation:

Try using a ball about the same size as the wide end of the funnels.

With an Adult

Brains over Brawn

Can you open a jar with a lid so tight even an adult can't open it?

Let's Find Out:

We'd all like to be strong, but some tests of strength are better met by *brains* than brawn.

What You Need:

A glass jar with a screw-on metal lid; a dish towel. *Optional:* rubber gloves.

What to Do:

1. Ask your adult helper to put the metal lid on a jar as tightly as possible. Tell your helper that no matter how tightly it's fastened, you'll be able to take it off!

2. Now try to loosen the lid of the jar. Unless you're as strong as your helper, you won't be able to loosen it.

3. Turn on the faucet so there's a thin stream of hot water coming out, and hold the lid end of the jar under the hot water. (To avoid burning your fingers, hold the jar by the bottom end and tilt it downward into the tap. You can use rubber gloves to hold it if you want.)

4. After a minute or so, remove the jar and turn off the water. Using a dish towel to grasp the lid, try opening the jar while the lid and glass are still warm. What happens?

What Did You See?

The metal lid was easy to remove after hot water had been run over it.

Why Did It Happen?

When metal gets hot, it expands or gets bigger. When glass gets hot it expands, too, but not as fast as metal. The metal lid expands faster than the glass jar, leaving space between the lid and the jar. Because the lid doesn't fit as tightly, it's easier to twist off.

Variation:

The next time your parents want to open a new jar from the pantry, ask if they'll let you try this new technique.

Look, No Mess!

Can you pull a newspaper out from under a glass of water—without spilling?

Let's Find Out:

Have you ever seen the old magician's trick of pulling a tablecloth out from under a full set of dishes, leaving the dishes in place? This is a beginner's version of the same trick! It uses the basic laws of physics and requires a quick hand—and some practice. You might spill a glass or two learning to do this, so check with your parents first about the best place to try it!

What You Need:

A plastic drinking glass with a *smooth* base; a perfectly smooth piece of newspaper with no seams.

What to Do:

1. Fill a plastic drinking glass half full with water, making sure the outside doesn't get wet.

2. Lay a long strip of newspaper on a dry, smooth part of the kitchen counter. (Right next to the sink might be the easiest to clean up in case you spill—ask your adult helper.) Set the glass of water on the paper.

3. Now practice by pulling *slowly* on the newspaper. Does the glass move with the paper?

4. Now for the real thing! Move the glass and newspaper a little farther back on the counter, and pull the newspaper from under the glass as *fast* as you can. What happens? Try it again!

What Did You See?

When you pulled the paper slowly, the glass of water moved with it. But when you pulled the paper very quickly, the glass stayed in place!

Why Did It Happen?

When pulled slowly, the paper and the glass stick together because of *friction*, and the glass moves with the paper. But pulling quickly breaks the grip of friction. Water makes the glass heavy, and heavy things tend to stay in one spot.

The heavier objects are, the more they stay put—*the law of inertia.* So, once the grip of friction is broken, the heavy glass stays in the same spot while the paper zips right out from under it.

Variation:

Try the same activity with an empty glass. Does it stay in place?

The Blob

Can you make a marble out of cooking oil?

Let's Find Out:

Have you ever looked at a container of salad dressing? The oil sits on top of all the other ingredients, and you must shake the dressing to mix them together. You can use this principle to make very unusual looking centerpieces for the dinner table. (But you wouldn't want to put them on your salad!) Make sure you have an adult helper for step 4.

What You Need:

A small (4-ounce or ⅛-liter) clear juice glass or jar with straight sides; food colorings; an eyedropper; a teaspoon; a sharp pencil; cooking oil; rubbing alcohol; tin foil or plastic wrap.

What to Do:

1. Start by filling a small glass about one-fourth full with water.

2. Add one drop of red food coloring to the water and stir.

3. With an eyedropper, make an oil blob on top of the water about 1 inch (2.6 centimeters) in size. (You might need to squeeze 2 to 4 eyedroppers full of oil.) Use the tip of a sharp pencil to connect any stray small drops to the large drop.

4. With your adult helper's assistance, tip the glass to one side and *slowly* pour rubbing alcohol down the side until the glass is half full. Add more alcohol until the drop of oil becomes a round ball and floats in the middle of the mixture. Cover the glass with tin foil or plastic wrap if you want to keep the mixture from evaporating.

What Did You See?

Oil floated on top of the colored water. When you added the rubbing alcohol, the oil drop formed a round ball and sank to the middle of the glass.

Why Did It Happen?

Oil is lighter than water and does not mix with it. When it floats on the surface, the oil is pressed flat by the air above it. Adding rubbing alcohol makes the water less thick, and the oil drop sinks. The alcohol-water mixture pushes on the oil drop evenly from all sides, forming it into a ball. Glass marbles are formed by dropping hot melted glass from a tall tower; the air pushes the glass into a perfect sphere and cools it at the same time.

Variations:

1. Try making oil marbles of various sizes.
2. Try coloring the water and alcohol with a different color.
3. Try making more than one oil marble in the solution.

Defying Gravity

Can you make water flow upward?

Let's Find Out:

You know that water doesn't flow uphill . . . it always flows downward because of the pull of gravity. One familiar exception to this rule is water that is under pressure, like water in a straw or the water that moves upward through the water pipes in your house. But there's another way to move water upward, too, and it's practically effortless.

What You Need:

Two clear plastic soft drink bottles the same size—16 ounces (½ liter) or smaller; a funnel; food coloring; a stiff index card (or envelope); a bowl.

What to Do:

1. Carefully fill one plastic soft drink bottle to the brim with hot water from the tap. (To avoid burning yourself, use a funnel to fill the bottle.)

2. Stand the bottle of hot water in a bowl on the kitchen counter, and add about 20 drops of your favorite food coloring. (A dark color works best.) Let the food coloring mix with the water.

3. Quickly fill the other soft drink bottle to the top with *very* cold tap water. (Don't put any food coloring in it!) Now put a stiff index card or envelope over the top.

4. With your adult helper's assistance, turn the cold bottle upside down, holding the card in place so the water doesn't leak out. Stand it upside down on top of the bottle filled with the colored hot water. Make sure the top bottle balances on the bottom bottle, but have your helper hold onto it to make sure it doesn't fall. Now carefully pull out the card, and watch what happens!

What Did You See?

The colored hot water flowed upward like smoke into the bottle of cold water. Gradually the cold and hot water mixed, creating warm water, all one color, in both bottles.

Why Did It Happen?

Heating water makes it expand and get lighter. Since it is lighter, hot water rises to the top while the heavy, cold water sinks to the bottom. Swimmers notice that the water at the bottom of a swimming pool, lake, or river is cooler than the water on the surface. Likewise, when sipping a cold drink with a straw, the coldest part is at the bottom of the cup.

Variation:

Try this again with colored cold water in the bottom bottle and clear hot water in the top bottle.

Upside-Down Water

Can you empty water from a glass without touching it?

Let's Find Out:

Usually you have to hold a glass of water upright to fill it with water and tip it over to empty the water out. But in this activity you'll keep a glassful of water *upside down* without any water leaking out—and then you'll empty the glass without touching it!

What You Need:

Two clear plastic drinking glasses of identical size; a dishpan or large bowl (a mixing bowl works well); a straw. *Optional:* a dime.

What to Do:

1. Fill the kitchen sink with a few inches of water. Then, fill two plastic drinking glasses with water by holding them beneath the surface. Make sure they fill completely.

2. The next step is tricky, so you might want to let your adult helper do it. Hold the rims of the glasses together, lift them out of the sink, and set them in the other side of a double sink or in a dishpan or large bowl. Be sure to keep the water from draining out of the top glass.

3. Move the top glass slightly so that the rims are just a little apart but the water still stays in. Can you think of a way to remove all the water from the top glass—*without touching either the glass or the bowl?*

4. The secret? Hold the end of a straw near the tiny space where the two rims are offset, and blow through the straw. What happens? Keep blowing until the top glass is empty.

What Did You See?

No water escaped from the glasses—even after they were offset—until you began blowing air through the straw. The air entered the crack between the two glasses and bubbled up inside the top glass, pushing some water downward and out through the crack.

Why Did It Happen?

Water molecules stick together, creating *surface tension* that makes the water surface stretch like a rubber band. That surface tension, plus the pressure of the air outside the glass, keeps the water from leaking out. Air is lighter than water, but it does take up space, so when you blow air into the glass it rises to the top and pushes some of the water out.

Variation:

Do you think you could place anything *inside* the filled glasses without losing any water? Carefully tilt the top glass just a *little* with one hand while you slip a dime through the crack with your other hand. What happens?

Why Blow It, Heat It!

Can you blow up a balloon—using heat?

Let's Find Out:

You can blow up a balloon using your lungs or a pump, and many stores that sell balloons blow them up with a tank of compressed air. But did you ever try to blow one up using the freezer and the stove?

What You Need:

An empty glass soft drink bottle; a balloon that has already been stretched or blown up; a saucepan.

What to Do:

1. Place an empty glass soft drink bottle in the freezer for about 15 minutes.

2. Remove the cold bottle and set it on the kitchen counter. Then, put a small well-stretched balloon over the top. Wait and watch as the bottle warms up to room temperature. What happens to the balloon?

3. Set the bottle and balloon in a saucepan half-filled with water. Put the pan on a stove burner, and have your adult helper pick a fairly low burner temperature to warm the pan.

4. Watch the balloon as the water warms. What happens? Heat the water until it's very warm—*not* boiling—and then turn the burner off. Don't remove the bottle until the water and pan have cooled. What happens to the balloon as the pan cools?

What Did You See?

The balloon puffed up as the cold bottle warmed to room temperature. It increased in size even more as you warmed the bottle in the pan of water.

Why Did It Happen?

When air is heated it expands, pushing what's around it. The hot air inside the bottle isn't strong enough to move the glass sides, so it goes out the top and inflates the balloon. The amount of air in the bottle doesn't change, just the amount of space it takes up. Likewise, large hot air balloons that carry people are filled with hot air from a propane blowtorch. The hot air inside the balloon, created by the blowtorch, is lighter than the cold air outside. Because it's lighter, the hot air lifts the balloon and attached gondola off the ground.

A Birthday Trick

Can you make it very hard to blow out a candle?

Let's Find Out:

How can you make it difficult (or impossible) to blow out the candles on a birthday cake? Well, you could buy some of the trick candles found in toy stores and gift shops. *Or,* you can try this simple method, using things you already have in the kitchen. Try it yourself, then try it on a friend!

What You Need:

A candle; a candleholder; a small funnel; matches. *Optional:* different-sized funnels.

What to Do:

1. Put a candle in a candleholder, and place it on the kitchen counter.

2. Have your adult helper light the candle (or do it yourself, if your helper says it's OK and supervises). Then try blowing out the flame. Any problem?

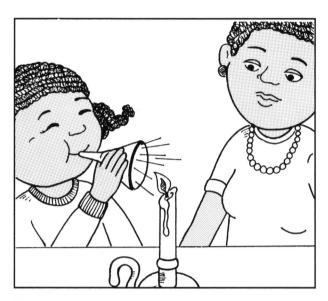

3. Light the candle again, and this time try blowing through a funnel, with the small end in your mouth. (Don't get the funnel in the flame!) What happens?

4. Now have your adult helper blow through the funnel while you watch the flame.

What Did You See?

You could blow out the candle easily until you tried blowing through the funnel! The flame actually looked like it was being blown toward the funnel, not away from it like you would expect.

Why Did It Happen?

Air tends to flow along a surface, so when you blow air through the funnel, it clings to the funnel's sides. Very little air travels through the center of the funnel. The faster-moving air along the sides of the funnel creates a low-pressure area in the center of the funnel. This phenomenon is called the *Bernoulli Principle* (see Against the Wind). The air on the opposite side of the candle rushes to this low-pressure area to equalize the pressure. This air pushes the candle flame toward the center of the funnel, not away from it.

Variations:

1. Try different-sized funnels.
2. Try blowing from the big end of the funnel.

Fireproof Paper

Can you fireproof a paper cup?

Let's Find Out:

Do you think you could hold paper over an open flame and *not* have it burn? It *can* be done, and this activity will show you how.

What You Need:

A candle; a candleholder; a paper cup (*unwaxed*); metal tongs; matches.

What to Do:

1. Place an unlit candle in a candleholder, and set it in the sink. Turn on the kitchen fan so the smoke alarm won't go off.

2. Fill a paper cup half full with water.

3. Have your adult helper light the candle (or do it yourself if your helper says it's OK and supervises).

4. Place the cup on the counter, and grasp it near the base with metal tongs. Hold it directly over the flame. Have your adult helper time you for two minutes. What happens? The cup is made of paper . . . isn't it?

What Did You See?

The cup turned black where the candle-flame hit it, but it didn't burn. No water leaked out—in fact, the water began to get hot!

Why Did It Happen?

The paper cup would get hotter and hotter and burst into flame if there wasn't any water in it. The water, however, absorbs the heat and keeps the cup cool enough not to burn. Water in the radiator of your family's car keeps the engine cool; without the water, the engine would get so hot that it could burn or even melt.

Variation:

Do you think you could *boil* the water in the cup? How long would it take? Try it!

The Rainmaker

Can you make it rain in your kitchen?

Let's Find Out:

We're all used to seeing it get cloudy and rain outside. But did you ever think what it would be like if it rained *inside,* too? That would get pretty messy! You can actually make rain *right in your own kitchen,* though, and if you and your adult helper follow the instructions, you won't even make a mess!

What You Need:

A saucepan with a lid; a pot holder; a metal pie plate; ice cubes; 2 oven mitts.

What to Do:

1. Put a saucepan half full with water on a stove burner smaller than the bottom of the pan.

2. Put the lid on the pan, and have your adult helper turn on the stove and bring the water to a boil. Your helper can tell you when the water is boiling—you'll see steam leaking out from under the lid. Using the pot holder, take off the lid and check.

3. Fill a metal pie plate with ice cubes—not *too* full (you don't want it to be too heavy)!

4. Have your adult helper use oven mitts to hold the pie plate over the pan of boiling water as you watch underneath. What do you see? (Now think about what happens to hot, moist air when it floats high into the sky and meets cold, dry air.)

What Did You See?

When you took off the lid, the boiling water made steamy water vapor that floated up and disappeared. But when the water vapor touched the ice-cold pie plate, tiny water droplets formed and fell like rain.

Why Did It Happen?

When the sun warms bodies of water, some of the water evaporates, cools, and forms clouds of water vapor. When the clouds get cool, the vapor *condenses* (becomes more dense) and falls to the earth as rain. (When the clouds get very cold, the water freezes and falls to the earth as snow.) Likewise, the boiled water in the saucepan evaporates to form a cloud of water vapor (steam). The steam that comes in contact with the cold pie plate condenses, forming rain.

The Invisible Fire Fighter

Can you put out fires using something invisible?

Let's Find Out:

You already know how fire fighters put out most fires—they use *lots* of water! But they put out fires with other things, too. In this activity you'll make a fire extinguisher that puts out fire—with something you can't even see!

What You Need:

A candle; a candleholder; a tall plastic drinking glass; a tablespoon (15 milliliters) measure; baking soda; a ¼-cup (60 milliliters) measure; vinegar; a long-handled spoon; matches. *Optional:* some soda pop; a cardboard tube (an empty toilet paper roll).

What to Do:

1. Place a candle in a candleholder, and set it in the sink. (The sink is one of the safest places to experiment with fire, because there's plenty of water available for putting the flame out quickly.)

2. Put a tablespoon (15 milliliters) each of baking soda and water in a tall plastic drinking glass. Stir the water and baking soda together with a long-handled spoon. What happens?

3. Next, add ¼ cup (60 milliliters) of vinegar. What do you hear . . . and see? The ingredients are mixing together to form bubbles of carbon dioxide gas. Don't worry about the gas floating out the top of the glass—it won't because it's heavy enough to stay in there.

4. Have your adult helper light the candle (or do it yourself if your helper says its OK and supervises). Pick up the glass and *slowly* tilt it toward the candle, so that the carbon dioxide gas pours onto the flame. (*Don't* pour the water, baking soda, and vinegar on the flame.) What happens? Make a new solution and try it again!

What Did You See?

The invisible carbon dioxide gas rolled out of the glass and put out the flame.

Why Did It Happen?

Fires need oxygen in the air to keep them burning. Because carbon dioxide is a heavy gas, it pushes away the oxygen the candle flame needs to keep burning, and the fire goes out. Carbon dioxide is used in fire extinguishers for putting out fires in homes, cars, and other places.

Variations:

1. To control the carbon dioxide gas better, try pouring it onto the flame through a cardboard tube (an empty toilet paper roll works well). Just be sure not to get the tube too close to the flame!
2. Carbon dioxide gas is found in soda pop, too—that's what makes the fizz. Try pouring soda pop in the candleholder below a small lit candle.

Cabbage Test

Can you tell how a food will taste . . . before you eat it?

Let's Find Out:

There are probably some foods you like to eat and some you don't. Did you ever wish you could tell how a food would taste before you even put it in your mouth? Many foods are either *acids* or *bases;* acids usually taste sour and bases usually taste bitter. If you want to know whether a food is an acid or a base without tasting it, you can make a purple dye that will tell you.

What You Need:

Red cabbage; a saucepan; a soup spoon; a strainer; a bowl; 3 plastic drinking glasses; clear (white) vinegar; baking soda; an eyedropper; a ¼-cup (60-milliliter) measure; a teaspoon (5 milliliter) measure. *Optional:* Grape, beet, or cranberry juice; other foods.

What to Do:

1. Have your adult helper heat some water in a teakettle until it boils. Use your fingers to tear 2 or 3 red cabbage leaves into little pieces, and put the pieces in a saucepan.

2. Have your adult helper pour just enough boiling water over the cabbage leaves to cover them. Let the cabbage soak for 15 to 30 minutes, stirring occasionally with a soup spoon.

46

3. Let the mixture cool, then have your adult helper give you a hand with pouring it through a strainer and into a bowl. Now you have your testing mixture . . . cabbage juice! (Be sure to refrigerate the juice when you're not using it, and don't spill it on your clothes—it'll stain!)

4. Now fill 3 separate glasses—the first with ¼ cup (60 milliliters) of water, the second with ¼ cup (60 milliliters) of white vinegar, and the third with water plus a teaspoon (5 milliliters) of baking soda. Using the eyedropper, put several drops of cabbage juice in each glass. What happens?

What Did You See?

When you added the cabbage juice to the plain water it stayed purple, but when you added it to the vinegar it turned red. When you dropped it in the solution of water and baking soda, it turned green!

Why Did It Happen?

Cabbage juice and many other fruit and vegetable juices contain a special chemical, called an *indicator*, that causes them to change different colors when mixed with an acid or base. Vinegar is an acid and baking soda is a base, so both change the color of the cabbage juice. Plain water is *neutral*—neither an acid nor a base—so it doesn't change the color at all.

Variations:

1. Try using grape, beet, or cranberry juice instead of cabbage juice.
2. Test other foods to decide whether they are sour acids or bitter bases—or neutral.

Tight Squeeze

Can you get a hard-boiled egg into a milk bottle—without pushing?

Let's Find Out:

Have you ever seen a model ship inside a glass bottle? How could it be squeezed through such a small opening? (Actually, it's not—it's put together inside the bottle!) But here you'll learn how to put a hard-boiled egg through the narrow neck of a bottle . . . in one piece and without pushing!

What You Need:

Several hard-boiled eggs (you may need to try this experiment several times!); a glass bottle with an opening just smaller than an egg (try a milk bottle, a flower vase, a wine decanter, a salad oil cruet, or a small baby bottle); butter (or margarine); paper; matches; metal tongs; a table knife.

What to Do:

1. Have your adult helper make several hard-boiled eggs. (This takes about 10 to 15 minutes.) Once the eggs have cooled, carefully take the shell off several of them.

2. Put butter (or margarine) around the opening of the glass container. Have your adult helper light a small match. Then have your helper pick up a small piece of paper with metal tongs, light the paper, and drop the burning paper into the bottle.

3. Quickly set the egg on the opening. What happens?

4. To retrieve the egg, rinse the bottle out with water so the burnt paper comes out first. Then turn the bottle upside down so the egg fits in the neck of the bottle. Blow into the bottle. If you're lucky it will squeeze back out! If not, try warming the neck of the bottle with water. (If all else fails, use a table knife to chop the egg up . . . then make an egg salad sandwich!)

What Did You See?

As the paper burned inside the bottle, the egg was pulled in.

Why Did It Happen?

Fire needs oxygen in the air to keep burning. As the paper burns, it uses up some of the air in the bottle; the remaining air gets hot and expands, and some slips out past the egg. The oxygen being burnt and the other air slipping out leaves less air inside the bottle . . . less *air pressure*. The stronger air pressure outside the bottle then pushes the egg in. Blowing into the bottle when removing the egg increases the air pressure in the bottle, which helps push the egg out.

Cut–or Not?

Can you cut an ice cube in half—and still leave it whole?

Let's Find Out:

When you cut a piece of paper in half, you get two pieces of paper, of course, and when you cut an apple in half, you get two pieces of apple. So how can you cut an ice cube in half . . . and still end up with a whole ice cube?

What You Need:

A plastic 2-quart (2-liter) soft drink bottle; a sharp knife; a cork that fits in the end of the bottle; metal tongs; 30 inches (75 centimeters) of very thin wire (30-gauge hobby and flower wire works well); 2 heavy 16-ounce (500-gram) food cans, unopened; pliers; an ice cube.

What to Do:

1. Fill a plastic soft drink bottle with water. Stand it on the counter, then test a cork to make sure it fits snugly in the bottle's mouth.

2. Have your adult helper use a sharp knife to cut a V-shaped slot in the top of the cork. (It's safest to hold the cork with tongs when cutting.) Put the cork back in the bottle.

3. Wrap some very thin wire around two food cans, leaving about 12 inches (30 centimeters) of wire between the cans. Wrap the wire around the middle of each can several times, and use pliers to twist it so it won't come loose.

4. Set an ice cube on the cork and lay the wire on the cube, directly over the slot in the cork. Let the cans hang down on both sides of the bottle. Push downward gently on the cans to cut the ice faster—it will take about 10 minutes for the wire to cut through the ice and land in the slot. Is the cube in one or two pieces? Why?

What Did You See?

The wire slowly cut through the ice cube, but the cube was still in one piece when the wire finally snapped into the slot in the cork.

Why Did It Happen?

The wire puts pressure on the ice, and the pressure causes heat that melts the ice. As the wire cuts downward the melted ice refreezes above it. (Some of the ice melts for good, though, because of the warm air temperature in the kitchen.) By the time the wire drops into the slot, the ice has frozen into one cube again. Ice skates work that way—the metal runners and the weight of the skater melt the ice, which becomes slippery, letting the skater glide smoothly, before it refreezes.

Air Power!

Can you crush metal with air?

Let's Find Out:

Holding your hand out a car window—or even sitting by the open car window—lets you feel the force of the rushing air. But even when you're standing quietly in the kitchen, air is pushing on every inch of your body . . . with about 15 *pounds* of pressure per square inch. If you find that hard to believe, try this experiment.

What You Need:

An empty aluminum soft drink can; a tablespoon (15 milliliters) measure; metal tongs; a large bowl.

What to Do:

1. Fill a large bowl almost full with cold water, and set it next to the stove.

2. Pour 1 tablespoon (15 milliliters) of water into an empty aluminum soft drink can. Place the can on a stove burner and have your adult helper heat the can until steam comes out the top for two minutes. *Don't touch the can with your hands* . . . it's very hot!

3. Have your adult helper grasp the can with metal tongs—keeping the hand facing palm up.

4. Then have your helper quickly turn the can upside down and place it into the bowl of water . . . it must be *straight up and down* when it hits the water. What happens?

What Did You See?

The can crumpled with a loud bang when it was placed in the water.

Why Did It Happen?

Heat makes the air inside the can expand and turns the water into vapor. The water vapor pushes the hot air out of the can. By the time the water evaporates, there is little air left in the can, and the air pressure is very low. Dipping the can into the water prevents it from taking in any more air to equalize the pressure—just like putting a lid on the can. The water cools the inside air, shrinking it and reducing the air pressure even more. The stronger outside air pressure pushes in on the walls of the can, crushing it instantly.

Wash Out

Can you make colors disappear?

Let's Find Out:

Kitchen chemicals are often useful, but sometimes they can even be magical. Laundry bleach, which contains a chemical called sodium hypochlorite, helps remove stains from clothes and other items. You can use this common chemical to create your own magic. Bleach is dangerous, though, so be sure to wear old clothes and have an adult helper assist you!

What You Need:

Two clear plastic or glass drinking cups; an eyedropper; washable ink (or blue food coloring); a plastic or metal spoon for stirring; a tablespoon (15 milliliters) measure; liquid chlorine bleach. *Optional:* other food colorings; liquid or powdered nonchlorine bleach.

What to Do:

1. Fill a plastic or glass drinking cup half full with water.

2. Using an eyedropper, put four drops of ink into the water, then stir with a spoon. (You can use blue food coloring instead, but the reaction will be slower.)

3. Have your adult helper fill a tablespoon (15 milliliters) with liquid bleach, and pour it carefully into another cup. Be sure not to get any bleach on your clothes or your skin!

4. Slowly pour half of the colored water into the cup with the bleach. What happens? Now it looks like plain water, but don't drink it! Keep adding more of the colored water. What happens? (Empty the cups and spoons and wash them all *thoroughly* as soon as you're done.)

What Did You See?

The bleach removed the color from the water!

Why Did It Happen?

Bleach is a *solvent* that dissolves, or breaks down, ink and food coloring. Its chlorine combines with hydrogen molecules found in the water. Then the other molecules found in water—oxygen—join with the chemicals that color the ink and change (*oxidize*) the chemicals, removing the color. Because bleach reacts with so many things, it must be handled very carefully—it should not be spilled on anything or mixed with any other chemicals unless you *know* it's safe to do so.

Variations:

1. Try other food colorings. Is the change as complete or rapid?
2. Fill one empty cup with bleach and another with water. Drop ink in both. What happens?
3. Use liquid or powdered nonchlorine bleach instead of liquid chlorine bleach. Do you notice any changes?

Bending Bones

Can you bend bones—without breaking them?

Let's Find Out:

Bending bones might not be as awesome as Superman bending steel bars, but it's almost as difficult. Most people who try it end up breaking them instead—just like what happens to a turkey wishbone. A common kitchen ingredient is the key to bending bones *without* breaking them.

What You Need:

Meat bones; ¼-cup (60-milliliters) measure; liquid bleach; tongs; 1-pint (or ½-liter) jar with a lid; vinegar.

What to Do:

1. Start by saving some meat bones from dinner—any kind will do. You might want to save different-sized bones.

2. Clean the bones carefully by washing them in water. Then let them set for a day in a 1-pint (½-liter) jar of water with ¼ cup (60 milliliters) of liquid bleach added. Have your adult helper assist you by pouring the bleach. Cover the jar.

3. Using tongs, take the bones out of the jar and rinse them under the tap. Can you bend them?

4. Put the bones into a jar of vinegar, screw the lid on tight, and let them set for 3 or 4 days. Take the bones out, rinse them, and try to bend them. If they aren't soft, put them back into the vinegar for several more days.

What Did You See?

The liquid bleach made the bones white. The vinegar made them soft and bendable.

Why Did It Happen?

The bleach removed color from the bones just as it removed color from the water in Wash Out. About two-thirds of a bone's weight is made of minerals such as calcium, phosphate, and carbonate. The rest of the bone is made of material consisting largely of protein strands called *collagen*. The vinegar (an acid) dissolves the calcium and other hard mineral parts of the bone. The soft protein parts, which bend without breaking, are left.

Steam Engine

Can you turn a teakettle into an engine?

Let's Find Out:

Most small kitchen appliances—for example, mixers, can openers, coffee grinders, and electric carving knives—are powered by small electric motors. But where does the electricity come from? Some of it comes from power plants that use *steam turbines.* Is steam really that powerful? See for yourself!

What You Need:

A teakettle; paper; scissors; a straight pin; a straw; plastic or electrical tape; an oven mitt.

What to Do:

1. Take a 5-inch (12.5-centimeter) square piece of paper, and use scissors to cut from each corner halfway to the center (about 2 inches or 5 centimeters). *Don't* cut all the way to the center!

2. Fold every other corner of the paper to the center, and hold them there while you carefully push a straight pin through them and into a straw. Adjust the paper pinwheel so that it turns easily when you blow on it. Have your adult helper wrap the sharp end of the pin in plastic or electrical tape.

3. Let your adult helper boil water in a teakettle. You'll know when it's boiling because steam will come from the spout.

4. Once the water is boiling, make sure the spout is pointed *away* from you, then use an oven mitt to hold the pinwheel above the steam in front of it. *Don't get your hand in the steam . . . it's HOT!* Try holding the pinwheel at different distances from the spout. Where does it spin the best?

What Did You See?

The pinwheel spun when you held it above the steam from the teakettle. It spun best when you held it farther away from the spout rather than close to it.

Why Did It Happen?

Boiling turns water to steam and then to water vapor. The steam rises fast and very forcefully, pushing on anything it comes in contact with—such as the pinwheel. That pressure makes the pinwheel turn. Used on a larger scale, steam is powerful enough to drive the huge turbines that create electricity or to power the engine of an old steam locomotive.

Stop That Pop

Can you "fix" popcorn so it won't pop?

Let's Find Out:

Making popcorn is simple, but understanding *why* it pops is a little more difficult! Heat alone isn't enough—that's why some kernels never pop, leaving grannies, nerds, or whatever you like to call them in the bottom of the bowl. So what is the secret to popping . . . or *not* popping?

What You Need:

One cup (¼ liter) of popcorn; a ¼-cup (60-milliliters) measure; a dish towel; a baking pan; a large saucepan with a lid; cooking oil; 2 jars; 3 large bowls.

What to Do:

1. Start by pouring a level ¼ cup (60 milliliters) of popcorn kernels into a jar. Cover the kernels with water, and let them stand for one day.

2. The next day drain the water, pour the kernels onto a towel, and blot them dry. Then put them in a dry jar labelled Soaked Popcorn.

3. Spread another level ¼ cup (60 milliliters) of popcorn kernels on a baking pan. With your adult helper's assistance, heat them in the oven for 90 minutes at 200°F (100°C). Let them cool, then place them in a jar labelled Heated Popcorn. Now you and your adult helper are ready to pop the different batches of kernels.

4. First, put 3 tablespoons (45 milliliters) of oil in a pan and pop the kernels you soaked in water. Remove the popped corn and set aside. Next, put more oil in and pop the kernels you heated in the oven. Then, add oil and pop a level ¼ cup (60 milliliters) of kernels right from the popcorn bag. Put each popped batch in a separate bowl and compare them. Which group has the most popped kernels? What's the secret to popping?

What Did You See?

Most of the kernels you soaked in water did not pop. The kernels you heated in the oven popped, but some looked slightly burnt. The popcorn straight out of the bag popped best and had the fewest unpopped kernels.

Why Did It Happen?

Popcorn has a secret ingredient—water.

When the kernel is heated, the moisture inside changes to vapor, which expands and pushes against the shell until it pops. The outer shells of water-soaked kernels get too soft to hold in the pressure until it builds up to an explosion. Oven-heated kernels lose some of their moisture through evaporation; it seeps out in the oven. Without this moisture, the kernels can't develop the steam pressure they need to explode until they are so hot some of them burn.

Crystal Candy

Can you make crystal candy from sugar?

Let's Find Out:

When you add sugar to Kool-Aid, lemonade, or ice tea it disappears or *dissolves*. Have you ever wondered where the sugar goes when you stir it into the water? An even tougher question is how could you get those tiny sugar crystals back? It's not easy, but it's fun—and you'll love the results!

What You Need:

Sugar; a 2-quart (2-liter) saucepan; a spoon for stirring; 1-cup (¼-liter) and ¼-cup (60-milliliter) measures; cotton string; scissors; a table knife; a tall, narrow clear glass jar; a flashlight. *Optional:* salt; baking soda.

What to Do:

1. Pour three ¼-cup (60-milliliter) measures of water into a saucepan and, with your adult helper's assistance, heat it to boiling.

2. Turn off the burner and slowly add 1 cup (¼ liter) of sugar, stirring as you add. Keep stirring and adding more sugar until you can see tiny pieces of sugar floating in the water that will not dissolve. (That means the water is a *supersaturated solution*—it won't hold any more sugar.)

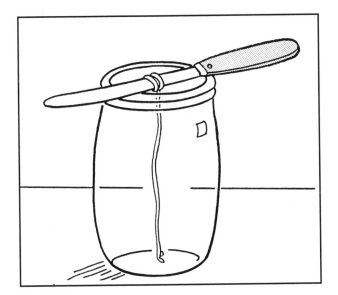

3. While the mixture cools, tie one end of a cotton string to the blade of a table knife. Hold the knife over a tall, narrow glass jar, and use scissors to cut the string where it would touch the bottom of the jar. (You can tie a knot at the bottom of the string to help it hang straight.)

4. When the mixture is cool, pour it into the jar, then rub some of the mixture and then some dry sugar on the string and drop the string into the jar. Put the glass in a safe, quiet spot and check it with a flashlight every day for 2 weeks. Try shining a flashlight through the glass onto the crystals to see them glitter. When you see rice-sized crystals on the string, remove the string, break off a crystal, and taste it!

What Did You See?

When the cloudy mixture of sugar and water cooled and sat for 2 weeks, it left sugar crystals on the string and on the top and bottom of the glass.

Why Did It Happen?

When sugar dissolves in water it doesn't really disappear. Actually, it breaks up into tiny sugar molecules too small to see with your eye. Hot water holds more sugar than cold water. So when the sugar water cools, it can't hold as much sugar, and some of the sugar forms crystals on the string.

Variations:

1. Try letting the glass sit until all the water evaporates.
2. Try making crystals with other kitchen ingredients like salt or baking soda.

Secret Messages

Can you send invisible messages?

Let's Find Out:

Did you ever want to write a secret note to someone . . . and make it *invisible*? Writing secret notes is fun, and you can do it using a simple ingredient from the kitchen cabinet. Just be sure to have an adult helper for the last step!

What You Need:

Vinegar (white or red); a small bowl; a small watercolor paintbrush or toothpick; white writing paper; two pairs of metal tongs. *Optional:* other liquids such as milk, lemon juice, or soda pop.

What to Do:

1. Start with the ingredient that makes invisible writing possible—vinegar. Pour a little vinegar into a small bowl.

2. Dip a paintbrush (or, if you don't have one, the large rounded end of a toothpick) in the vinegar, and write a message on a piece of white paper. Write just a few words or numbers.

3. Set the paper aside, and let the vinegar dry completely. Can you see the message?

4. Turn on the kitchen fan and, with your adult helper's assistance, use metal tongs to hold the paper over an electric stove burner on low or medium heat or in front of an electric iron. Hold the paper very close to the burner, but don't let it touch! Watch carefully as the paper gets warm. What happens?

What Did You See?

The vinegar dried clear and invisible on the white paper. But the heat from the stove made the letters turn brown so you could see them.

Why Did It Happen?

Vinegar, fruit juices, and other liquid foods contain carbon compounds that turn brown quickly when heated. The liquids start to burn and get brown before the paper does. Many solid foods do the same thing, though you can't write with them (this process is what makes bread turn brown in the toaster).

Variations:

Try using other liquids to make more invisible notes—for example, milk, lemon juice, or soda pop. Which works the best?

Tornado

Can you make a tornado in a bottle?

Let's Find Out:

Did you ever notice how water draining from a full sink or bathtub creates a little whirlpool? If you could see it from the side, it would look very much like the tornadoes that sometimes accompany severe storms. Do you think you can make one of these little tornadoes . . . in a *bottle*?

What You Need:

Two 2-quart (2-liter) clear plastic soft drink bottles with caps; a nail; a ballpoint pen; plastic or duct tape. *Optional:* food coloring, glitter.

What to Do:

1. Screw the lid on one soft drink bottle. Have your adult helper poke a small hole in the middle of the lid with a nail, then enlarge the hole with a ballpoint pen. The hole should be at least ⅜ of an inch (about 1 centimeter) in diameter.

2. Remove the lid, and fill the bottle three-fourths full with tap water. Then screw the lid back on the bottle.

3. Stand an empty soft drink bottle upside down on top of the bottle filled with water. Don't use a cap on the empty bottle! Carefully tape the bottles together where they join. Use plenty of tape to make it a watertight connection!

4. Turn the bottles upside down so that the water-filled bottle is on top, and set them on the kitchen counter. Swirl the water in the top bottle until it gets moving in a circular motion. Then sit back and watch!

What Did You See?

At first, very little water dropped into the empty bottom bottle from the water-filled top bottle. After you stopped swirling the bottles, the water continued to swirl more rapidly. A hole opened up in the center of the water, and the water drained into the bottom bottle. The swirling water resembled a tornado.

Why Did It Happen?

Because water is heavy, it has the potential to make things move. Once you put water into motion by swirling it, gravity continues to pull it downward. This rotation of the water, combined with the pull of gravity, forces the water to the sides of the container—creating a hole in the center of the water above the hole in the lid. The water forms a tornado.

Variations:

1. Try swirling the water in the opposite direction.
2. Color the water with food coloring, or add glitter to it.

The Spy

Can you see around a corner—with a milk carton?

Let's Find Out:

You don't need Superman's X-ray vision to see what's around a corner or behind a tree. You can do both of these things— or just be snoopy—by turning a milk carton into a periscope.

What You Need:

A milk carton (1 quart or 1 liter); scissors or a sharp knife; two rectangular pocket mirrors (2-by-3 inches or 5-by-8 centimeters); duct tape.

What to Do:

1. Carefully open the top of an empty milk carton. Wash and dry the carton—you don't want a smelly periscope!

2. With your adult helper's assistance, use scissors or a knife to carefully cut a 1-by-1-inch (2.6-by-2.6-centimeter) hole at the center top on one side of the carton and the center bottom of the opposite side.

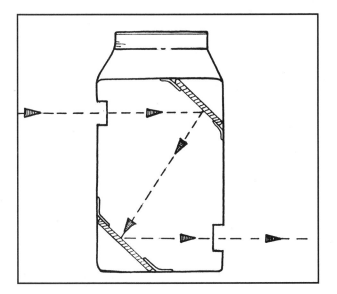

3. Tape two mirrors inside the carton, one at the top and one at the bottom. The mirrors should be tilted at 45° angles, with the shiny sides facing each other. You might need some assistance from your adult helper to get the mirrors in the right positions.

4. Tape the top of the carton closed and look through either hole. What do you see? Can you look around a corner? Out a window? Over the top of the sofa? Under the bed?

What Did You See?

The mirrors reflected images to your eyes, making it possible to see around corners and behind things.

Why Did It Happen?

The mirrors are tilted so that light coming from one direction bounces or reflects from one mirror up (or down) to the other mirror and then into your eye. Sailors in submarines use periscopes to see ships on top of the water.

Variation:

Could you make a periscope two or three milk cartons high? Would the angles of the mirrors have to change?

Alien Garden

Can you grow a garden *without* seeds?

Let's Find Out:

Most gardens have plants that grow from seeds you plant in the soil. But you can grow a garden without planting seeds at all! Of course it doesn't look like a typical garden—in fact, it looks like something you might see on another planet!

What You Need:

A glass pie plate (metal might corrode); some small pieces of porous rock; some charcoal or coal; twigs; an old sponge, cut up into small pieces; a jar; a tablespoon (15 milliliters) measure; ammonia; liquid laundry bluing; salt; a spoon; food coloring; a magnifying glass.

What to Do:

1. Take a glass pie plate, and put some twigs and small pieces of rock, charcoal (or coal), and sponge in it. Scatter them about.

2. With your adult helper's assistance, mix the following in a jar: 2 tablespoons (30 milliliters) of ammonia and 4 tablespoons (60 milliliters) each of liquid bluing, salt, and water. The mixture stinks—don't breathe it!

3. Pour the mixture evenly over the objects in the pie plate. Don't splash it on yourself! Use a spoon to scoop out any salt left in the jar, and scatter it on the objects.

4. Put a few drops of food coloring on the items in the pie plate. Then put the pie plate in a safe place where the liquid can evaporate. Your garden must remain at room temperature so keep it out of direct sunlight. Check after several days. Look through a magnifying glass . . . what do you see?

What Did You See?

The chemicals formed *crystals* in the pie plate—lots of them. These crystals looked different from the crystals you see in rocks such as granite or quartz.

Why Did It Happen?

Crystals, though they look and grow like plants, are not alive. Salt crystals form when a salt solution evaporates. As each new crystal forms, it develops tiny spaces through which the salt solution is drawn out to the edges of the crystal. As the solution evaporates, it leaves another crystal stacked on top of the first. The process continues until all of the solution evaporates. As clusters of salt crystals form, they attach to tiny spaces in solid objects, such as the small holes in charcoal, coal, twigs, and porous rocks.

Variation:

Mix another batch of ammonia, laundry bluing, salt, and water, and add it to the pie plate once the first batch has evaporated.

KIDS PICK THE FUNNIEST POEMS

compiled by Bruce Lansky

illustrated by Steve Carpenter

Kids call it "the funniest poetry book I've ever read" and say it's "funnier than TV." (One kid said, "I laughed so hard I fell out of my chair.") The reason: a panel of 250 elementary school children helped Bruce Lansky pick the 80 funniest poems from over 500 poems written by the world's funniest poets, including Shel Silverstein, Dr. Seuss, Jack Prelutsky, Judith Viorst, Jeff Moss, and Ogden Nash, as well as relative unknowns.

The poems are accompanied by 75 black & white illustrations by Hallmark Cards' creative director, Steve Carpenter. Bruce Lansky is the author of the best-selling *Dads Say the Dumbest Things!* and is the #1 author of baby name books. Hardcover. **#2410**

FREE STUFF FOR KIDS

by the Free Stuff Editors

America's #1 children's activity book, with over 2.5 million copies in print.

Exciting new items include:

- Major League baseball, NBA & NHL team "fan packets" that include stickers, photos, and schedules
- Environmental information like Jacques Cousteau's *Dolphin Log* and *Animal Agenda* magazines, recycling fact sheets, and a "Keep America Beautiful" coloring book
- Teenage Mutant Ninja Turtles, Barbie, and Nintendo stickers
- *Surprises* magazine
- An American flag wall poster.

#2190

Order Form

Qty.	Title	Author	Order #	Price	Total
	SCIENCE BOOKS BY JIM LEWIS:				
	Hocus Pocus Stir & Cook, Kitchen Science		2380	$7.00	
	Learn While You Scrub, Science in the Tub		2350	$7.00	
	Measure Pour & Mix, Kitchen Science Tricks		2370	$7.00	
	Rub-a-Dub-Dub, Science in the Tub		2270	$6.00	
	ADDITIONAL BOOKS BY MEADOWBROOK:				
	Almost Grown Up	Patterson, C.	2290	$4.95	
	Dads Say the Dumbest Things!	Lansky/Jones	4220	$6.00	
	Dino Dots	Dixon, D.	2250	$4.95	
	Discipline w/out Shouting/Spank	Wyckoff/Unell	1079	$6.00	
	Do They Ever Grow Up?	Johnston, L.	1089	$6.00	
	Free Stuff for Kids, 15th Ed.	FS editors	2190	$5.00	
	Grandma Knows Best	McBride, M.	4009	$5.00	
	Kids Pick the Funniest Poems	Lansky, B.	2410	$13.00	
	Moms Say the Funniest Things!	Lanksy, B.	4280	$6.00	
	Parents' Guide Baby & Child Care	Hart, T.	1159	$8.00	
	Practical Parenting Tips	Lansky, V.	1179	$7.00	
	Ready for School?	Eberts/Gisler	1360	$5.95	
	Sand Castles Step-by-Step	Wierenga	2300	$6.95	
	Weird Wonders/Bizarre Blunders	Schreiber	4120	$4.95	

Subtotal	_____
Shipping and Handling	_____
MN residents add 6.5% sales tax	_____
Total	_____

YES! Please send me the books indicated above. Add $1.50 shipping and handling for the first book and 50¢ for each additional book. Add $2.00 to total for books shipped to Canada. Overseas postage will be billed. Allow up to four weeks for delivery. Send check or money order payable to Meadowbrook Press. No cash or C.O.D.'s, please. Prices subject to change without notice. **Quantity discounts available upon request.**

Send book(s) to:

Name _____ Phone (___) _____

Address _____

City _____ State _____ Zip _____

Payment via:

☐ Check or money order payable to Meadowbrook Press. (No cash or C.O.D., please.) Amount enclosed _____

☐ Visa (for orders over $10.00 only.)

☐ Master Card (for orders over $10.00 only.)

Account # _____

Signature _____ Exp. Date_____

A FREE Meadowbrook Press catalog is available upon request.
You can also phone us for orders of $10.00 or more at 1-800-338-2232.

Mail to: Meadowbrook Inc., 18318 Minnetonka Blvd., Deephaven, MN 55391

(612) 473-5400   Toll-Free 1-800-338-2232   FAX (612) 475-0736